Research on Investigate Social Media Impact On Entrepreneurship Development

Social Media Impact On
Entrepreneurship *Development*

Table of Contents

No	Title	Page No
01	Executive Summary	03
02	INTRODUCTION	05
03	Rational of the study	06
04	Impact of the Internet on Strategy	07
05	Literature review	08
06	Objective of the study	09
07	Methodology of the study	13
08	Analysis and interpretation of the data	16
09	Findings of the study	21
10	Conclusion	23
11	Recommendations	23
12	References	24
13	Appendix (Questionnaire)	25

EXECUTIVE SUMMERY

Through this research our main goal is to find out "How social media transformed into a great business landscape to the entrepreneurs" and "How entrepreneurs are getting benefited from this". In the past social media usually used for on entertain purpose where the user only used many other social media platforms to amuse themselves but now a day's people do use social media for marketing and selling business products also. So it's a great transform for utilizing the platform for entrepreneurs.

Many young entrepreneurs use various platforms of social media to introduce and selling their products to the customer through this. In fact thorough our research and other sources we find out many of the consumer find it comfortable and easy to buy from online rather go into shopping malls. And of course the new entrepreneurs who are usually fresher finds it easy to use various social media platform as their market place, because it takes less effort and capital to start. In the data analysis part we can see many of the new and existed entrepreneurs are

comfortable on those social media because of it doesn't need much of a capital and promotional activities

In this research we have identified what kind of impact has been placed to the new entrepreneur's development. We have also find the entrepreneurs think Facebook and Instagram are the two major platforms that helps them to get their business started.

Our research shows answers of mainly two questions, which is a how social media impact positively on entrepreneurship development? And how social media save time and money to develop entrepreneurship?

Many of the entrepreneur's thinks through social media they can stay connect with their customers, their brand and products are more exposure by those platforms and the marketing of their products is easy to get the customers attention.

INTRODUCTION

In the previous period of time social media used for only communication with friends and entertainment, but now a day the use of social media has change. Many people start their business through social media as a result fresher and student get a new platform for their business. In online business it is not necessary to manage a huge amount of investment, people can involve in this kind of business with a minimum amount which they can effort. Social media develop entrepreneurship in many ways. Many young entrepreneurs specifically are exploiting the gathering of people and potential virility of the huge swath of mediums to spread the news for better outcomes, and longer-enduring activities. For our shopping and marketing social media is most important, in this pandemic situation it's not only important its essential. Our country is a developing country. Every year a lot of student completes their graduation from public and private university, they have qualification but there is a very short of job market in our country. As a result, unemployment rate is increase day by day. This problem can be solved by social media business. Social media can develop entrepreneurship and decrease unemployment problem.

RATIONALE OF THE STUDY

∅ Why we have chosen this particular research

For our topic of research, we have chosen to focus on the main objective of the research is to identify social media impact on entrepreneurship development by considering current situation and advantages of media. In this covid-19 situation people shouldn't go outside for shopping and other works, but in case of emergency they can go for their urgent. In this pandemic situation social media platform or online marketing takes a very important role instead of offline market. Now a day many entrepreneurs start online business for their profit, because people are getting use to buy product from online. Customers are not felling safe shopping or buy anything outside from their home. Not only in this situation social media helps us to buy a product from online in normal condition, and many of people like who recently complete their graduation or student they are start involve with this kind of social media business. As a result, unemployment problem is decreasing day by day

∅ What question we want to answer

After completing our research, we took mainly two questions; the first question is how social media impacts positively on entrepreneurship development? And the second question is how social media save time and money to develop entrepreneurship?

∅ How we will find the best source.

In finding information to answer our research questions, we try to find out how social media impact for an entrepreneurship development now a day, and what is its benefit. Survey will help us for collecting data which important for us to investigate our research. In our research, we will collect primary data through questionnaire.

❖ Impact of the Internet on Strategy – A Model for Web 2.0?

Porter considered the impact of the internet on strategy and how it might inform as to Web 2.0's likely impact. Porter (2001) states that many people thought that the internet would make strategy redundant, but argues that the reverse is true. He is critical of those who thought that the internet would provide first-mover advantage it did not as switching costs were lower, not higher and the promised benefit of network effects did not materialize at first. The latter has now been realized e.g. eBay (Kumar, 2004). The web, the 'third knowledge revolution' after printing and broadcasting, has either eroded or nullified competitive advantage traditionally enjoyed by firms (Wilson & Gilligan, 2005) or any advantage that it might have offered is neutralized by its mass adoption by companies (Porter, 2001). Piercy (2002) suggests that "strategy is redundant" (p.206) because of the speed of change brought about by the internet. As a consequence of the web, we should "redefine strategy as the art of surviving rapid transition" (Evans & Wurster, 2000; Piercy, 2002, p.206).

LITERATURE REVIEW

Social media platforms (for example, Facebook, Snap-chat and Instagram) are increasingly accepted as vital to the day-to-day lives of millions of users who interact in virtual environments. This new way of communication continues to dominate the cultural landscape and impacts on how users do business.

On the other hand, the rapid development of technology and intense rivalry between businesses has meant that the business community is continuously searching for new ways to distinguish themselves and provide value to clients. Social media is a phenomenon that has been facilitated by the age of the Internet and a rise in the general usage of digital media. It has motivated businesses to engage with different corporate segments and has driven many towards the adoption of innovative modes of interaction.

There are many businesses of small and medium enterprises running by individuals now converting their advertising management on Internet through face book and you tube etc. For the betterment of the business and their products promotion social media is considered very fruitful and helpful because it creates direct relation with the masses and they can leave their comments to make better product according to their requirement. It is considered that social media not only attracts to the existing customers but it also grabs the attention of the potential customers to develop their interest about their product.

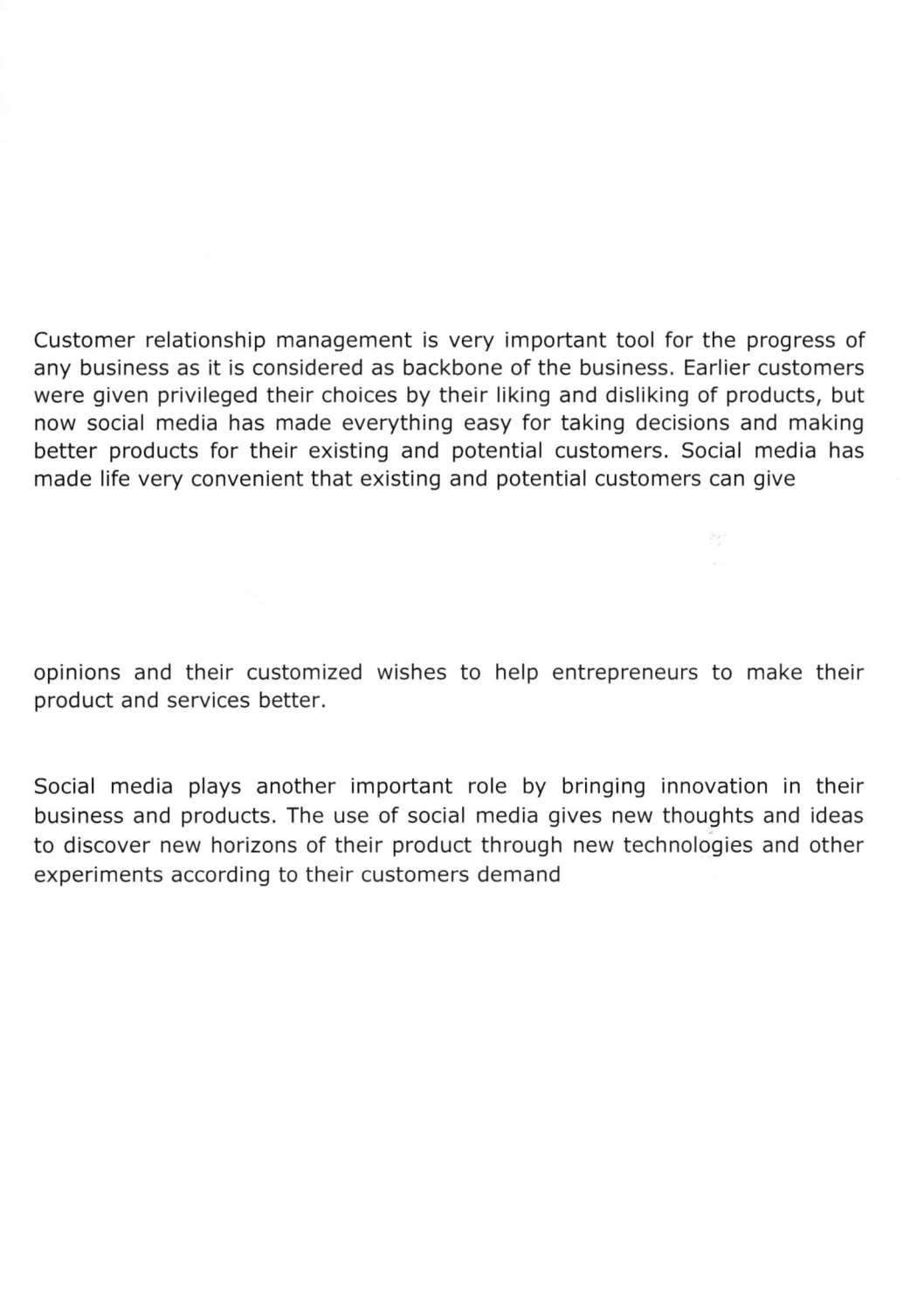

Customer relationship management is very important tool for the progress of any business as it is considered as backbone of the business. Earlier customers were given privileged their choices by their liking and disliking of products, but now social media has made everything easy for taking decisions and making better products for their existing and potential customers. Social media has made life very convenient that existing and potential customers can give

opinions and their customized wishes to help entrepreneurs to make their product and services better.

Social media plays another important role by bringing innovation in their business and products. The use of social media gives new thoughts and ideas to discover new horizons of their product through new technologies and other experiments according to their customers demand

OBJECTIVE OF THE RESEARCH

Social media has greatly transformed the business landscape. It is one of the most important aspects of digital marketing, which provides incredible benefits that help reach millions of customers worldwide.

Objective of the research are:

Ø☐ Create an Omni Channel customer service

Today's customers choose social media as the main source to interact with a brand as they get instant attention. Research says that 42% of consumers expect a response on social media within 60 minutes. Social media is a powerful channel to engage customers who reach out to you through different social media channels such as Facebook, Twitter, Linked-In, Instagram, and Whats-app to deliver a seamless Omni channel messaging experience.

Ø☐ Reach out to the bigger audience

Almost 90% of marketers say their social marketing efforts have increased exposure for their business, and 75% say they've increased traffic. It an ideal way to create brand awareness and stay in contact with the customers. Social media platforms are becoming the main source for people to learn more about businesses latest information about new products, services, advertisements, deals or promotions.

- Ø☐ Segment the audience
- Ø☐ Make use of visuals
- Ø☐ Initiate conversations
- Ø☐ Measure the efforts
- Ø☐ Works on the SMM

Many businesses are jumping into the Social Media Marketing (SMM) bandwagon as its positive impact on brands and promises profitable success when done properly. Social media marketing techniques target social networks and applications to spread brand awareness. Social media marketing is perceived as a more targeted type of advertising and therefore it is very effective in creating brand awareness. Social media engagement campaigns produce a lot of shares; generate more views and publicity for the business all for a one-time cost.

- Ø☐ **Improves user engagement**

No matter businesses are on social media or not, customers follow their social media accounts every day. With the average person spending just under two hours per day on social media, social media engagement is essential to make sure your brand is capturing enough attention. Setting up a social media presence, building and engaging them effectively with quality content is a big effort. But the biggest benefit a company can glean from your investment in social media is to reach out to your potential customers wherever they can be found across the globe. Social media engagement is positive as the reputation it generates for your brand but on the other hand, a single negative tweet can bring bad publicity overnight, which is difficult to reverse. Below are a few best practices for engaging users.

∅☐ Make a Social customer service

Providing stellar customer service is likely already a top priority for every business. But along with the two-way communication that social media provides, it also offers a unique opportunity to step up the customer service game and provide instant gratification to our target audience. Whatsapp, for example, is the most popular channel for customer service on a global front. The numbers say there are more than 1.5 billion monthly active users, sharing more than 60 billion messages every day, a huge amount of on-platform activity. Whatsapp Business app, launched by Whatsapp enables business users to "interact with customers easily by using tools to automate sort and quickly respond to the messages.

✓ Specific Objective:

- To identify the factors of social media induce entrepreneur and what's the reason behind this.
- To identify why entrepreneur selected social media to run business
- How satisfied the entrepreneur's are with social media service
- Why entrepreneurs chosen social media

✓ Objective of the research approach to the problem:

- Creating a cohesive brand image can be difficult
- It's not easy to erase the mistake
- It can be problematic to measure social media ROI.
- Becoming overly dependent on social media
- Negative customer reviews can cause dama

✓ General objective:

The objectives of the report are to analyze the social media impact on entrepreneurship development.

METHODOLOGY OF THE RESEARCH

Ø Type of research:

Data analysis has done using quantitative research, which is used to establish the data and which are used to evaluate the accuracy of the results, obtained. Research problem can be stated through questionnaire method that ultimately helps to success our research.

Ø Sources of Data:

We have collected data from questionnaire to respondents who are users of social media.

Ø Data collection procedure:

We have used quantitative method. We have collected our data for this report in one ways, such as: primary data through survey and for doing the survey, we have prepared a questionnaire on investigate social media impact on entrepreneurship development. We have observed the opinions that are users of social media.

Ø Questionnaire:

We have collected our data through questionnaire, the questionnaire conducted based on primary data. Primary data collected through questionnaire survey. The structured questionnaire containing both open and close ended was used. A survey through a standardized questionnaire was conducted to collect quantitative information from users of social media.

- **Population:**

Total population of this research study comprises of all the university students aged 20-30 years, who have access to Internet and users of social media.

- **Variables of the study:**

Exposure to social media is independent variable and attitude and behavior are dependent variable. As the study based on likert survey model.

- **Sample Size:**

This study consists of a sample size of 25 respondents, because of the time limitation of our research.

- **Data analysis and reporting:**

Quantitative data were collected and analyzed the different pie chart are used to make the data meaningful.

- **Research Technique:**

Just percentage is used to analyze the data.

Five Smart Ways to Use Social Media to Grow Your Business in 2019

1. Use social media to drive traffic to your e commerce stores.

2. Use plenty of videos on social media to keep your audience engaged and growing.

3. Build brand awareness by using targeted influencers on social media to market your products for you.

4. Provide massive amounts of value before asking for anything in return.

5. Use social media to tell your brand story and successfully differentiate yourself from the competition.

DATA ANALYSIS AND INTERPRETATION

After collecting all the data from the respondent, we analyzed data by following ways:

The way we used to collect data is a survey format where we created a questionnaire for our respondent. We have followed qualitative methods for data collection. Data analysis is the process of interpreting the meaning of the data, which we collected and organized in the form of pie chart and other representation.

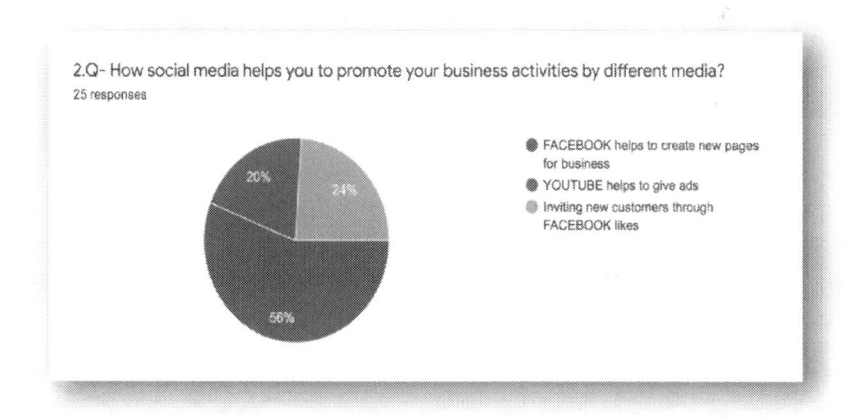

2.Q- How social media helps you to promote your business activities by different media?
25 responses

- FACEBOOK helps to create new pages for business
- YOUTUBE helps to give ads
- Inviting new customers through FACEBOOK likes

20%
24%
56%

In this pie chart it shows that social media help people to promote their business with the help of different media. Among the 25 respondents, the majority of the respondent agrees that FACEBOOK helps to create new pages for business. On the contrary, some respondent agrees that YOUTUBE helps them to give ads of their products. In this situation social media should create new ways or scope for the entrepreneur so that they can easily run their business and solve their unemployment problem as well as.

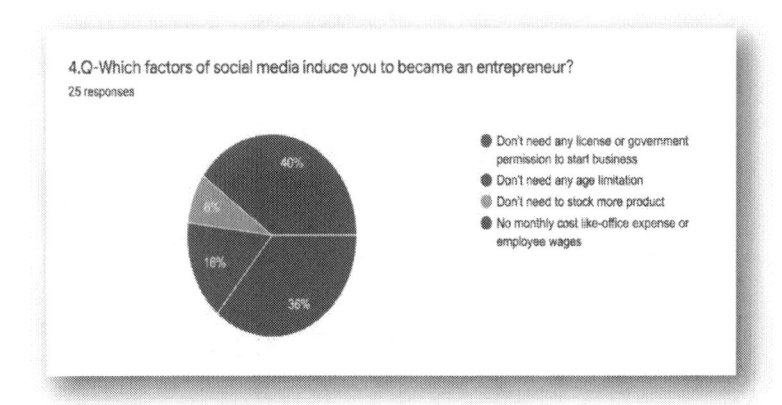

4.Q-Which factors of social media induce you to became an entrepreneur?
25 responses

- Don't need any license or government permission to start business — 40%
- Don't need any age limitation — 36%
- Don't need to stock more product — 6%
- No monthly cost like-office expense or employee wages — 18%

Respondent have given information that the factors behind entrepreneurship is that there is no monthly cost like-office expense or employee wages. On the contrary, some respondent agrees that, they don't need any license or government permission to start business. So social media should create more easy and accessible platform so that the entrepreneurship can be developed and increase entrepreneur.

6.Q- As an entrepreneur why you have selected this media to conduct your business?
25 responses

- Don't need much capital: 52%
- Don't need much budget for Promotional activities: 48%
- Required less educational background

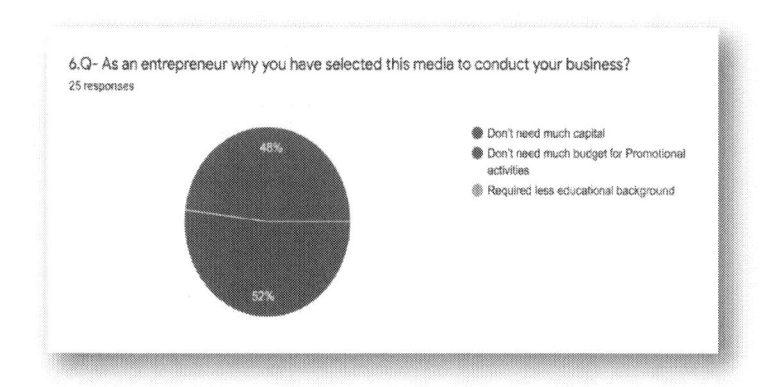

This pie chart shows why entrepreneur have selected social media to conduct business, majority of the respondent said that they don't need much capital for starting a business. Some of the respondent agrees that they don't need much budget for promotional activities.

Social media need to increase more facilities for the entrepreneur so that they can expand their business and utilize the facilities of social media fully.

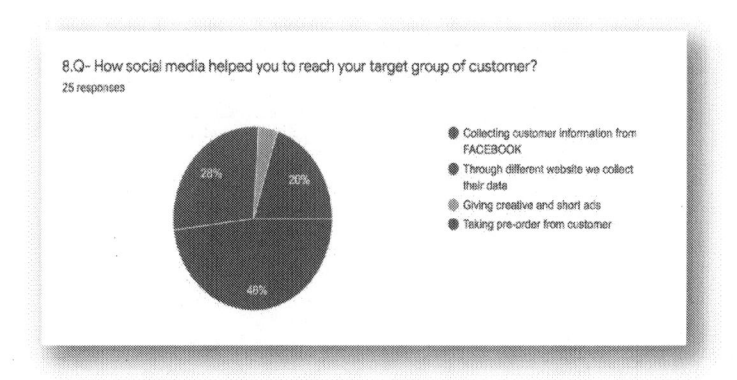

8.Q- How social media helped you to reach your target group of customer?
25 responses

- Collecting customer information from FACEBOOK — 48%
- Through different website we collect their data — 28%
- Giving creative and short ads — 20%
- Taking pre-order from customer

This pie chart represents how entrepreneur reach their target group of customer and among the 25 respondent 48% said that they collect customer information from FACEBOOK. And the rest of the respondent said that they reach customer by collecting information from different website.

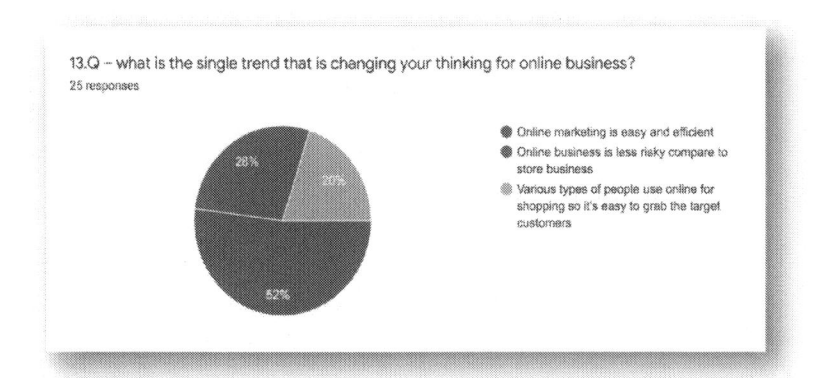

13.Q – what is the single trend that is changing your thinking for online business?
25 responses

- Online marketing is easy and efficient
- Online business is less risky compare to store business
- Various types of people use online for shopping so it's easy to grab the target customers

28%
20%
52%

This chart represents which factors or benefits have change entrepreneur thinking for online business, here among the 25 respondent 52% said online marketing is easy and efficient. And the rest of the respondent agrees that online business is less risky compare to store business.

FINDINGS OF THE STUDY

After analyzing all the chats and opinion of the respondent we got some shorts of issues, they are given below-

- Social media is helping new entrepreneur to start new business in online.

- Entrepreneur's think that conduct business in online doesn't need much capital or government permission.

- Social media helps to save money for promotional activities.

- The survey also shows that reaching target group of customer is easy when entrepreneurs use online platform.

- New ideas can be executed through online business can be less risky whether if they conduct it physically then it can be higher risk.

- Social media requires fewer budgets to use it for business where physically conducting a business requires huge budget.

- Loyalty of the customer can't be gain easily through online business whether a consumer buying products face to face can be more loyal.

- Though social media helps entrepreneur's development but it has some negative effect on those entrepreneurs who are doing business without virtual environment.

- Social media motivating people to solve their unemployment problem by starting new business in online.

CONCLUSION

Social media used for only communication with friends and entertainment. But many people start their business through social media as a result fresher and student get a new platform for their business. And I think this is the right way to use social media.

RECOMMENDATION

- Ø Social media can develop entrepreneurship and decrease unemployment problem.
- Ø Unemployment rate is increase day by day. This problem can be solved by social media business.

REFERENCES

1) Abi-Aad, G. (2015). Social Media for Social Entrepreneurship https://www.entrepreneur.com/article/249379 Accessed 7 July 2017

2) Debrand, M. (2016). How Social Media Influences Consumer Purchasing Decision. https://markdebrand.com/social-media-purchasing-decision/. Accessed 7 July 2017

3) Kaplan, A] and Haenlein, M. (2009). The fairyland of Second Life: Virtual social worlds and how to use them. Business Horizons 52 (6), 563-572.

4) Samuel, B. S. and Joe, S. (2016). Social Media and Entrepreneurship. The Social Sciences. 11(15), 639-644

APPENDIX

QUESTIONNAIRE FOR SURVEY

1. Q-Social media create new ways for conducting business in online platform for new entrepreneur.

   i. Yes
   ii. No

2. Q- How social media helps you to promote your business activities by different media?

   i. FACEBOOK helps to create new pages for business
   ii. YOUTUBE helps to give ads
   iii. Inviting new customers through FACEBOOK likes

3. Q-Why it's easy to start new business on social media?

   o Less costly
   o Easy and fast to communicate
   o Don't need any extra space or warehouse to keep product
   o Above the all

4.Q-Which factors of social media induce you to became an entrepreneur?

i. Don't need any license or government permission to start business o Don't need any age limitation

ii. Don't need to stock more product

iii. No monthly cost like-office expense or employee wages

iv. Above the all

5. Q-Do you think social media positively impact on entrepreneurship?

i. Yes
ii. No

6.Q- As an entrepreneur why you have selected this media to conduct your business?

i. Don't need much capital

ii. Don't need much budget for Promotional activities

iii. Required less educational background

6. Q-As an entrepreneur, how satisfied you are with social media service

i. Satisfied
ii. Dissatisfaction
iii. Very dissatisfied

8.Q- How social media helped you to reach your target group of customer?

i. Collecting customer information from FACEBOOK
ii. Through different website we collect their data
iii. Giving creative and short ads
iv. Taking pre-order from custom

9.Q – why do entrepreneurs decide to use social media for their new business?

i. Easy to grab the customers attention
ii. Easy to grab consumers through innovative marketing
iii. Can create a vast community

10. Q – Can social media marketing really helps to grow business?

i. Yes
ii. No

11. Q – Does blogging on social media helps to get the target consumer
i.   Yes
ii. No

12. Q – Is social media marketing better for B2C and B2B.

i. Agree
ii. Strongly Agree
iii. Strongly disagree

13. Q – what is the single trend that is changing your thinking for online business?

i.   Online marketing is easy and efficient
ii. Online business is less risky compare to store business
iii. Various types of people use online for shopping so it's easy to grab the target customers

13. Q – Do you think social media is the most sought after method adopted by new entrepreneur?

i. Agree
ii. Disagree

15. Q – Does social media most effective solution for brand promotion?
i.   Yes
ii. No

16. Q- which social media network helps to the new entrepreneur?

i. Facebook
ii. Youtube
iii. Linked-in
iv. Twitter
v. Most of the above

17. Q- Do you think social media marketing will help for entrepreneur to find their potential customers?

vi. Yes
vii. No
viii. May be

18. Q- what benefits is entrepreneur getting through social media marketing?

i. Brand awareness
ii. Bring attention to promote
iii. Better customer loyalty and trust
iv. Strengthen customer service

19. Q- Why has new entrepreneurs chosen social media?

i. Better customer reach
ii. Lesser price
iii. Global expansion
iv. Research and learning

20. Any suggestion would you like to give for the better use of social media?

Made in United States
Orlando, FL
25 August 2022